THE WEST PHILADELPHIA BILLIONAIRES SOCIETY

A Blueprint for Community-Owned Wealth and Prosperity

AARON MAXWELL MONTAGUE

The West Philadelphia Billionaires Society
A Blueprint for Community-Owned Wealth and Prosperity

Published by:

Kingdom Publishing
1350 Blair Drive, Suite F
Odenton, MD 21113

Printed in the United States of America

Copyright ©2025 by Aaron Montague

ISBN: 978-1-967006-09-0 (Paperback)
ISBN: 978-1-967006-10-6 (Ebook)

Table of Contents

Foreword

Every generation is given the opportunity to dream—and then to decide whether those dreams will be left as ideas or built into living legacies. What you hold in your hands is not just another book filled with inspiring words. This is a blueprint. It is a call. It is a strategy rooted in both faith and vision for how communities can rise together.

As I read through these pages, I felt the urgency and the conviction that echo throughout. The West Philadelphia Billionaires Society is not a metaphor—it is a movement. It dares to imagine what happens when everyday people commit to extraordinary unity. It dares to replace poverty with possibility, despair with dignity, and broken systems with bold ownership.

What strikes me most about this work is its integration of spiritual truth with economic empowerment. The author rightly reminds us that ownership is not simply about dollars—it is about destiny. Stewardship is not just financial—it is biblical. And when we align our faith with our finances, our prayers with our plans, heaven and earth converge to create transformation that cannot be denied.

This book gives us a vision of what happens when we stop waiting for a savior to rescue us and instead realize that the power has been in our hands all along. A dollar a day. A million united voices. Businesses, schools, hospitals, media platforms, and banks owned not by outsiders, but by the very people they serve. That is not fantasy. That is the future being written right here.

I commend this work to you—not just as a reader, but as a participant. These words will challenge you. They will stir your faith. And they will call you to action. Because this is more than a book to admire. It is a plan to adopt. It is a movement to join. It is a covenant to walk in together.

My prayer is that as you turn each page, you will not only see the problems of our world more clearly, but also see yourself as part of the solution. Let this vision grip your heart, awaken your mind, and stir your spirit. For when we build together, no mountain is too high, no system too broken, and no future too far.

Welcome to the West Philadelphia Billionaires Society. Welcome to a movement that declares: *we are not beggars, we are builders; we are not renters, we are owners; we are not victims, we are visionaries.*

The blueprint has been given. Now, let's build.

—Bishop Dr. Antonio M. Palmer, D.Div
Kingdom Alliance of Churches International

The Call of a Million Voices

I want you to picture this with me. Close your eyes if you must. See it not just with your eyes but with your spirit. Imagine walking down the streets of West Philadelphia, where once the corner was claimed by despair, but now the corner store is owned by the people. Imagine the gas station where you fill your tank—it no longer drains dollars out of our neighborhood but circulates wealth back into our homes. Imagine the hospital where your grandmother receives care, the bank where your son gets his first loan, the school where your daughter learns not only history but how to own her future—all owned, operated, and sustained by us.

This is not fantasy. This is not a dream deferred. This is not "someday." This is now. This is the prophetic summons of what I call the West Philadelphia Billionaires Society (WPBS).

Why West Philadelphia?

West Philadelphia is not just a dot on the map. It is a story, a song, a testimony of survival and resilience. It is where rhythm meets soul, where culture meets creativity, where innovation has always been born, even in the cracks of oppression. It is a place that has birthed scholars, singers, entrepreneurs, leaders, athletes, preachers, warriors, and dreamers.

But it is also a place that has carried the scars of systemic neglect, redlining, underfunding, and over-policing. A place where potential has too often been buried under the rubble of poverty and violence. Yet, out of this very ground, out of this very soil—rich with the blood, sweat, and tears of our ancestors—God has planted a vision.

West Philadelphia is not just the beginning point; it is the blueprint. What starts here can spread across America, and across the world. What rises here will echo in Detroit, Baltimore, Chicago, Kingston, Accra, Lagos, Port-au-Prince, and beyond.

Why Now?

Because time is not neutral. Because delay is death. Because every day, poverty drains, violence robs, hopelessness chokes, and division devours. Because too many of our sons are being buried, too many of our daughters are being abandoned, too many of our elders are being neglected.

And yet—listen closely—right now we are living in a divine convergence. Technology has made collective funding possible at the push of a button. Social media has given us the ability to gather voices like never before. The hunger for justice, equity, and ownership is rising like a tide.

We have been waiting for a hero, a savior, a benevolent donor. But what if the hero we've been waiting for is not one man, not one billionaire, not one politician? What if the hero is us? What if the hero is a million of us—each with $1 a day, pooled, multiplied, and focused into community ownership?

The Vision

The West Philadelphia Billionaires Society is not a charity. It is not a nonprofit that survives on grants and good intentions. It is a movement of ownership. Imagine it as a community mutual fund, where one million participants commit $1 a day—not as a donation, but as an investment. That's $30 million a month. That's $365 million a year. In ten years, that's over $3.6 billion.

And what happens with that wealth? We buy. We build. We own. Gas stations. Mini-marts. Grocery stores. Banks. Hospitals. Schools. Housing developments. Technology firms. Green energy. Entertainment hubs. Media platforms. We control the eight mountains of influence—business, family, education, religion, civics & government, healthcare, media, arts & entertainment.

We pay dividends back to the people. Not welfare, not charity, but ownership. True, measurable, bankable equity.

The Subconscious Call

And I want you to feel this deep in your subconscious. Because this is not just about money—it's about meaning. Not just about buildings—it's about belonging. Not just about ownership—it's about overcoming centuries of being owned.

Every dollar you invest becomes a declaration: We are not powerless. We are not waiting for crumbs. We are not beggars at the table of America. We are builders, owners, stewards, and visionaries.

Say it with me now—even if only in your mind:

"I am part of the million. I am part of the movement. I am part of the miracle."

Let those words echo inside you like a drumbeat, because repetition births conviction, and conviction births action.

The Spiritual Foundation

Make no mistake—this is not just economics. This is spiritual. The Bible declares, "The earth is the Lord's, and the fullness thereof; the world, and they that dwell therein" (Psalm 24:1). Ownership is not foreign to faith; it is a command. Stewardship is the proof of faithfulness. The parable of the talents (Matthew 25) is not just a story about money—it is a story about responsibility.

We are called not to bury our treasure in the ground but to multiply it. We are called not to consume all we have but to leave an inheritance for our children's children (Proverbs 13:22). We are called to be lenders, not borrowers, above only and not beneath (Deuteronomy 28).

WPBS is not just a business plan. It is a kingdom strategy.

Why You?

You might be asking yourself, Why me? Why now? My friend, because the world has been waiting for you. You are not here by accident. You are not reading this by coincidence. Something in your spirit has been yearning for a plan, a pathway, a people to connect with. You have been tired of talk with no action, promises with no proof, hype with no harvest.

This book, this vision, this movement is your answer. And you are the answer it has been waiting for.

The West Philadelphia Billionaires Society needs you—not just your dollar, but your voice, your hands, your ideas, your connections, your prayers, your faith. One million united voices will shake this nation to its core.

The Blueprint Ahead

In the chapters that follow, I will show you:

- The true cost of violence and poverty in our community.
- The extraordinary power of collective micro-investment.
- The eight mountains we must climb and control.

- The way to build businesses we own together.
- How dividends of dignity transform families and futures.
- The governance model that resists corruption and breeds transparency.
- How to replicate WPBS beyond Philadelphia to the African diaspora and the world.

Each chapter will be a revelation. Each story will be a mirror. Each strategy will be a seed. And as you read, you will not only learn with your mind, you will be moved in your heart, and you will be stirred in your subconscious to act.

A Prophetic Snapshot

So let me paint you a picture of what is to come. Twenty years from now, a child will walk through West Philadelphia. She will see stores, banks, hospitals, schools—all stamped with the seal of community ownership. She will not just hear about wealth on TV, she will live it in her own zip code. She will not have to leave her community to find opportunity; opportunity will live on her block.

And when she asks her grandmother how it all began, her grandmother will say: "It started when one million of us gave one dollar a day. It started when we believed that together, we could be billionaires."

The Invitation

And so, I invite you now—not just to read, but to join. Not just to nod your head, but to lend your hand. Not just to be inspired, but to be involved. Because this is more than a book—it is a blueprint. And blueprints are not meant to be admired; they are meant to be built.

Welcome to the West Philadelphia Billionaires Society.
Welcome to a new way of living.
Welcome to the miracle of a million voices.

Chapter 1
The True Cost of a Single Murder

The night was heavy with silence, the kind of silence that follows chaos. Blue and red lights flashed against the cracked brick walls of rowhouses. Mothers stood on porches, clutching their chests. Children peeked through curtains, eyes wide with the kind of fear they should never have to know. And there, on the cold pavement of West Philadelphia, lay Jamal.

Jamal was only nineteen. He had a laugh that could break through the darkest mood. He had dreams bigger than his block, bigger than his zip code. He wanted to design sneakers, to open his own store, to give his momma a house with a porch where she could sit in peace. But those dreams spilled into the street that night, along with his blood.

The headlines called it another homicide. The detectives called it gang-related. The city called it a statistic. But Jamal was not a statistic. Jamal was a universe — and when a universe collapses, it pulls everything around it into a black hole.

The Ripple Effect

Jamal's murder did not end with Jamal. The true cost of a single murder never does. His mother, once the anchor of her family, collapsed under the weight of grief. Her health declined. Her job performance plummeted. Depression wrapped around her like chains. His younger sister, once an honor-roll student, began failing her classes. She couldn't concentrate, couldn't sleep, couldn't dream. His friends, stunned with grief and burning with anger, looked for someone to blame, someone to retaliate against. The cycle prepared to repeat itself, one bullet birthing the next.

And beyond his family and friends, the entire neighborhood felt the aftershock. Property values dropped. Businesses hesitated to invest. Families whispered about moving away. Fear took root, and with fear comes withdrawal — neighbors retreating inside, shutting their doors, locking their trust.

The Economic Toll

But the cost of Jamal's death was not just emotional; it was economic. The city dispatched police, ambulances, detectives. The courts prepared for trial. The prisons waited for another young man caught in the cycle of vengeance. Each murder costs a city millions of dollars in emergency response, legal fees, incarceration, lost wages, and lost productivity.

Think about it: Jamal, had he lived, might have created a business, hired ten employees, served a thousand customers. Instead, the city must now spend upwards of $1.5 million in the aftermath of his death. Multiply that by the hundreds of murders in a single city each year, and you begin to see the economic hemorrhage.

Violence is not just a tragedy; it is a tax. It is a hidden, unvoted, involuntary tax that bleeds our community dry. And the poorest neighborhoods, already stripped bare, pay the highest rate.

The Generational Toll

Jamal's absence is now a permanent presence. His children, if he had lived to have them, will never be born. His mother's grandchildren will never know his laugh. His sister will never bring her brother to her wedding. Generations are altered, futures are erased, branches of the family tree cut off before they ever sprouted leaves.

And what is lost cannot be measured only in dollars or statistics. The true cost is generational. Every murder steals potential from the next century. Every bullet fired into the body of a young man ricochets into the future of his family.

The Spiritual Toll

The Bible tells us that the blood of Abel cried out from the ground (Genesis 4:10). Jamal's blood cries out too. It cries out for justice, for change, for redemption. Every murder is a wound in the spirit of a community. Every body that falls is not only flesh but faith collapsing, hope crumbling, belief in tomorrow evaporating.

Satan comes to steal, kill, and destroy (John 10:10). And murder is his masterpiece. He steals Jamal's future. He kills Jamal's body. He destroys Jamal's family. And when left unchecked, he convinces the community that this destruction is inevitable, that nothing can change, that we are powerless to stop it.

But he is a liar.

A Mirror for Us All

Let us not pretend Jamal is someone else's son. Jamal is ours. Jamal is your nephew, your neighbor, your student, your choir member. Jamal is the young man who held the church door open on Sunday morning, the boy who ran errands for his grandmother, the friend who made everyone laugh at the basketball court.

When one Jamal dies, we all lose. And if we do not calculate the cost, if we do not confront the loss, then we will keep paying the bill over and over, year after year, generation after generation.

The NLP Truth

Now, as you read these words, I want you to notice something. You can feel it in your chest, can't you? That tightening, that ache, that mix of anger and sadness. That is your subconscious signaling you: This cannot continue. And with every breath you take right now, you are engraving into your spirit a deeper truth: We can stop this.

Say it quietly, but firmly:

"We can stop this. We will stop this. We must stop this."

The mind moves toward what it repeats. Let this repetition sink beneath the surface of your conscious thought. Let it take root in the soil of your soul. Because change begins first in belief, and belief begins in repetition.

The Hidden Math

Here's the staggering reality: if one murder costs a city $1.5 million, then ten murders cost $15 million. A hundred murders cost $150 million. In cities like Philadelphia, Baltimore, Chicago, where homicides number in the hundreds each year, the true cost of murder easily reaches into the billions.

Now imagine what we could build if those billions were redirected— not into prisons, but into schools. Not into police overtime, but into business ownership. Not into funerals, but into futures.

What if the money currently spent cleaning blood off sidewalks was instead spent planting gardens in empty lots? What if the billions used to lock our sons away were instead invested in their ideas, their inventions, their enterprises?

The Prophetic Question

The true cost of a single murder is not only in the moment—it is in the echo. The echo that shakes the walls of homes, schools, and neighborhoods. The echo that ripples through time, stealing futures we will never see.

So here is the prophetic question: How much longer will we pay this bill? How much longer will we stand by as our wealth, our children, our future is drained by violence?

The Setup for the Blueprint

This is why WPBS matters. Because we cannot afford another Jamal. We cannot afford another mother's tears, another sister's despair, another father's absence. We cannot afford the emotional toll, the economic toll, the generational toll, the spiritual toll.

The West Philadelphia Billionaires Society is not just about making money—it is about stopping the bleeding. It is about replacing the cost of death with the profit of life. It is about ensuring that Jamal's story is not repeated, but redeemed.

Closing Refrain

So let us declare it:

- No more wasted lives.
- No more stolen futures.
- No more silent suffering.
- No more Jamals.

The cost is too high. The time is too short. The need is too urgent.

And so we move, we build, we act.

Because the true cost of a single murder is everything—and everything is exactly what we refuse to lose.

Chapter 2
Dollars With A Destiny

Imagine this: you hold a single dollar in your hand. Just one. The same crumpled bill you might have spent on a bag of chips, a soda, or a lottery ticket. Most of us don't even feel the loss of a single dollar. We misplace them in couch cushions, let them slip out of our pockets, toss them into donation jars without a second thought.

But what if that dollar had a destiny?

What if, instead of disappearing into the abyss of impulse purchases, that dollar became a seed? What if it joined hands with the dollars of your neighbors, your family, your community, until together they became a mighty river of wealth?

One dollar by itself is fragile. But one million dollars moving in the same direction is unstoppable.

The Avalanche Principle

You've seen a single snowflake fall. Harmless, delicate, almost laughable. But gather enough snowflakes together on a mountaintop, and you have the power of an avalanche — a force that can reshape the entire landscape.

That is what happens when we decide that our dollars are no longer aimless, but assigned. No longer wandering, but weaponized. No longer wasted, but working.

This is the destiny of the dollar in WPBS. It is no longer a snowflake. It is the beginning of an avalanche.

The Math of Destiny

Let me show you how ordinary dollars become extraordinary destiny.

- 1 person. $1 a day. That's $30 a month. $365 a year.
- 1,000 people. Now we're talking $365,000 a year. Enough to buy land. Enough to seed a credit union. Enough to launch a community business.
- 10,000 people. $3.65 million a year. That's hospitals, apartment complexes, franchises, scholarships.
- 100,000 people. $36.5 million a year. That's banks. That's supermarkets. That's renewable energy plants.
- 1,000,000 people. $365 million a year. Billion-dollar impact in less than three years.

That's not a dream. That's not hype. That's not impossible math. That's simple multiplication. That's what happens when we align our dollars with destiny.

NLP Anchoring — Feel It Now

I want you to do something with me right now. Take a deep breath in. Hold it. Exhale slowly. Now picture your own hand holding a single dollar. See it clearly. Feel the texture of the paper, the ink pressed into it. That dollar is not meaningless. That dollar is a soldier waiting for assignment.

Say this with me:

"My dollar has a destiny. My dollar is a seed. My dollar will multiply."

As you repeat it, you are programming your subconscious mind to see money not as something that leaves you, but as something that works for you. This is not just positive thinking. This is spiritual alignment. This is mental reprogramming. This is destiny in action.

The Curse of Aimless Dollars

For too long, our dollars have been slaves. They leave our communities and never return. Every time we buy from businesses that do not reinvest in us, our dollars are exiled. They work for someone else's children, someone else's future, someone else's dream.

In many communities, the dollar circulates 7 to 20 times before leaving. In ours? Less than once. That is financial genocide. That is silent robbery. That is destiny denied.

But the moment we reclaim our dollars and redirect them toward ownership, they break free. They return home. They serve our children, our schools, our streets.

The Power of a Collective Yes

One person saying, "I'll invest a dollar a day" is powerful. But one million people saying it together is revolutionary.

Think of a choir. One voice can sing a song. A thousand voices can fill a cathedral. A million voices can shake a nation. When we say yes collectively, the vibration cannot be ignored. Banks will hear it. Politicians will hear it. The world will hear it.

And the sound of that yes will be the birth cry of the West Philadelphia Billionaires Society.

Biblical Foundation of the Dollar Seed

Jesus told a parable of a mustard seed. The smallest of seeds, yet when planted, it becomes the largest of garden plants, even providing shelter for the birds (Matthew 13:31-32). A dollar a day is our mustard seed. Small, yes. But when planted in fertile soil, when watered with discipline, when nurtured with vision, it grows into a tree large enough to shelter generations.

Deuteronomy 8:18 reminds us: "But thou shalt remember the Lord thy God: for it is He that giveth thee power to get wealth, that He may establish His covenant." Wealth is not evil; it is divine empowerment. And our dollars, aligned with destiny, become covenant wealth.

Destiny vs. Distraction

Every dollar you spend is a vote. A vote for your future, or a vote for your distraction. A vote for ownership, or a vote for dependency. A vote for your children's inheritance, or a vote for your children's struggle.

When you hand over your dollar without purpose, it drifts into distraction. But when you assign it to WPBS, it is no longer a vote wasted. It becomes a declaration: I believe in collective wealth. I believe in shared ownership. I believe in destiny.

Subconscious Command — See the Future

Close your eyes for a moment. Imagine it is 10 years from now. You are walking down Lancaster Avenue. Where once there were abandoned storefronts, now there are businesses owned by the people. Where once you saw despair, now you see prosperity. And you know—deep down—you helped build this. Your dollars did not disappear. They multiplied. They transformed. They lived their destiny.

Breathe that in. Let it anchor in your subconscious. Because what you vividly imagine, you subconsciously pursue. And what you subconsciously pursue, you inevitably manifest.

The Refrain of Destiny

Let this be your refrain, whispered to yourself day and night:

- My dollar has a destiny.
- My dollar is a seed.

- My dollar will multiply.
- My dollar will build futures.
- My dollar will not be wasted.

The repetition of this refrain will rewire your financial consciousness. You will no longer see money as scarce, but as abundant. You will no longer see yourself as a spender, but as an investor. You will no longer see your dollar as small, but as significant.

The Setup for What's Next

Chapter 1 showed us the devastating cost of a single murder. Chapter 2 reveals the multiplying power of a single dollar. The contrast is intentional. Every murder drains millions. Every dollar invested generates millions. Every loss weakens us. Every seed strengthens us.

The question before us is simple: Will we keep paying the cost of death, or will we start investing in the profit of life?

Closing Declaration

Say this aloud, right now, as a declaration of faith and destiny:

"I refuse to waste another dollar. I refuse to watch my money leave my community. My dollar is a seed. My dollar has a destiny. My dollar will build the future. I am part of the million. I am part of the movement. I am part of the miracle."

And let that declaration echo not only in your mouth but in your mind, not only in your conscious thought but in your subconscious core.

Because destiny does not wait. And neither will we.

Chapter 3
The 8 Mountains We Must Climb

Have you ever stood at the base of a mountain and looked up, wondering if you had the strength to climb it? The mountain looks intimidating, towering above, wrapped in clouds, daring you to attempt the impossible. But here's the truth: mountains were never meant to intimidate us. Mountains were meant to be climbed. And when you stand on top of a mountain, you don't just own the view — you own the influence.

Our community has been kept at the bottom of too many mountains. But the West Philadelphia Billionaires Society is not about staying low. It is about rising up, climbing, conquering, and planting our flag at the summit. These are not mountains of stone and rock. They are mountains of power and influence. And there are eight of them.

Why Mountains?

The Bible tells us, "Whoever says to this mountain, 'Be thou removed, and be thou cast into the sea,' and shall not doubt in his heart, but shall believe that those things which he saith shall come to pass; he shall have whatsoever he saith" (Mark 11:23). Jesus spoke of mountains as obstacles, but also as symbols of authority. Mountains determine rivers. Mountains shape weather. Mountains command attention.

If we do not climb them, others will. If we do not claim them, others will. And whoever stands on top dictates what flows down.

The Eight Mountains of Influence

The framework is simple but profound. There are eight primary arenas that shape every society, every culture, every generation. If we want to transform West Philadelphia — and beyond — we must take ownership of these eight mountains:

1. Business
2. Family
3. Education
4. Religion
5. Civics & Government
6. Healthcare
7. Media
8. Arts & Entertainment

1. Business — The Mountain of Provision

Business is the engine that drives wealth. Without ownership of businesses, we are perpetual consumers, never producers. Right now, too many of the dollars we spend are captured by businesses that do not belong to us, do not reinvest in us, and do not care about us.

To climb this mountain, WPBS will launch co-ops, franchises, and community-owned enterprises. Gas stations, mini-marts, supermarkets, banks — owned by us, serving us, profiting us. When we own business, we own provision. When we own provision, we own power.

2. Family — The Mountain of Legacy

The strength of any community begins in the home. Strong families birth strong leaders. Weak families multiply cycles of poverty and violence. Our families have been fractured by incarceration, by addiction, by poverty, by systemic design.

WPBS will invest in family support systems, childcare centers, parenting programs, marriage strengthening, and youth mentorship. Because when we heal the family, we heal the foundation.

3. Education — The Mountain of Knowledge

Education is supposed to be the ladder out of poverty. But in too many of our neighborhoods, the ladder is missing rungs. Underfunded schools, outdated curriculums, and ignored students have stolen futures.

Through WPBS, we will fund scholarships, build tutoring programs, invest in STEM labs, and open community learning centers. Our children will not only learn history, they will learn ownership. They will not only study for jobs, they will be trained to create jobs. Because knowledge is not just power — knowledge is wealth.

4. Religion — The Mountain of Spirit

Faith has always been the heartbeat of our community. Churches have been safe havens, rallying points, and centers of hope. But too often, faith has been disconnected from economics. We shout on Sunday and struggle on Monday.

WPBS will partner with churches, mosques, and synagogues to align spiritual power with financial empowerment. We will teach that stewardship is worship, that ownership is obedience, that wealth creation is kingdom business. The mountain of religion must be reclaimed so our faith fuels our future.

5. Civics & Government — The Mountain of Justice

Policies shape neighborhoods. Laws determine opportunities. Leadership decides resources. And too often, our voices have been drowned out by money that buys influence.

21

But money has a voice. When WPBS commands billions, we will not beg politicians; we will summon them. We will sit at the table, not as beggars but as partners. We will advocate for policies that protect our children, fund our schools, and support our businesses. We will raise leaders from our own ranks to occupy offices, not just to pass laws but to pass legacies.

6. Healthcare — The Mountain of Healing

Our people die younger, sicker, and poorer. From preventable diseases to lack of access, healthcare has become a death sentence for too many.

WPBS will climb this mountain by funding clinics, supporting hospitals, and investing in wellness programs. We will train and employ our own doctors, nurses, and health workers. We will reclaim health as a right, not a privilege. Because healing is wealth.

7. Media — The Mountain of Narrative

Whoever controls the story controls the people. For too long, the media has portrayed our communities as crime scenes, our sons as threats, our daughters as stereotypes.

We must own the platforms — newspapers, radio, television, social media channels. We must create content that uplifts, informs, and inspires. We must tell our own stories, define our own image, and control our own narrative. Media is not just about information; it is about imagination. And imagination fuels destiny.

8. Arts & Entertainment — The Mountain of Influence

Music, movies, sports, fashion — they shape culture more than laws do. Our culture is imitated worldwide, yet we profit least from it. Our artists entertain millions, but too often die broke, exploited by contracts they didn't control.

WPBS will climb this mountain by building studios, production houses, and entertainment companies that we own. Our creativity must pay us, our influence must benefit us, our art must sustain us. Because when you shape culture, you shape the world.

NLP Reframe — From Helpless to Heroic

Now pause. Think of these mountains again. At first, they may feel overwhelming. But as you picture them, I want you to see yourself already climbing. See your community standing at the summit. Hear the sound of our flag being planted. Feel the wind on your face as you stand on top, looking down not with fear but with victory.

Say this with me:

"We are climbing. We are conquering. We are claiming the mountains."

Repeat it until you feel the shift. Because what you repeatedly confess, you inevitably create.

Biblical Echo

Caleb stood at 85 years old and said, "Give me this mountain" (Joshua 14:12). He did not ask for the easy land, the flat land, the soft land. He asked for the mountain, because mountains hold the high ground.

We are not asking for crumbs. We are asking for mountains. And through WPBS, we will climb them, one dollar at a time, one business at a time, one generation at a time.

The Setup for Chapter 4

The eight mountains show us where to climb. But climbing requires tools, strategy, and strength. That's where WPBS functions as our community's mutual fund. Together, we will not just dream of mountains — we will fund the climb.

Closing Declaration

Let us declare it together:

- We will climb the mountain of Business.
- We will climb the mountain of Family.
- We will climb the mountain of Education.
- We will climb the mountain of Religion.
- We will climb the mountain of Civics & Government.
- We will climb the mountain of Healthcare.
- We will climb the mountain of Media.
- We will climb the mountain of Arts & Entertainment.

Eight mountains. One people. One movement. One destiny.

Chapter 4
A Community Mutual Fund

Picture this with me: a group of ordinary people gather around a kitchen table. Each one pulls a dollar from their pocket. Alone, the dollar can't do much. But together, they push their dollars into the center of the table, and suddenly that table is covered. What looked small in their hands now looks powerful in the pile.

This is the vision of WPBS — not charity, not handouts, but a mutual fund for the people, by the people, owned by the people.

What Is a Mutual Fund?

In Wall Street terms, a mutual fund is a pool of money collected from many investors to buy stocks, bonds, and other assets. Instead of investing alone, you invest together. Instead of risking everything on one company, you spread your investment across many. It is safer. It is stronger. It is scalable.

Now imagine taking that same concept and applying it not to Wall Street, but to our street. Imagine one million of us pooling our dollars, not to make corporations richer, but to build what our communities desperately need: gas stations, supermarkets, hospitals, housing developments, technology firms, media outlets, entertainment hubs.

This is not theory. This is strategy. This is our community mutual fund.

The Dividend of Dignity

In traditional mutual funds, you get dividends — a payout of profits earned by your collective investment. WPBS operates the same way, but with a difference. Our dividends are not just dollars — they are dignity.

Every time you receive your share, it is proof that you are not a beggar, not a borrower, but an owner. It is proof that you have equity, that you have stake, that you are building a legacy.

Think of it: you open your mailbox or your bank app and see your dividend payment. It is not charity. It is not welfare. It is ownership. It is your money working for you, your family, your community.

And the greatest dividend is not just what hits your account — it is what happens in your mind. You begin to see yourself not as powerless, but as powerful. Not as a consumer, but as a shareholder. That shift in mindset is the true wealth.

Metaphor: One Brick at a Time

Building a community-owned empire is like building a fortress. No single brick can stop the storm. But when you lay brick upon brick, row upon row, wall upon wall, suddenly you have a fortress that can withstand any attack.

Each dollar you contribute to WPBS is a brick. By itself, it seems small. But laid next to another, and another, and another — soon you have walls of wealth, towers of opportunity, gates of security.

How It Works — The Simplicity of Systems

Let me break it down clearly:

- You contribute $1 a day. That's $30 a month. $365 a year.
- Your dollar joins millions of others. Together, we pool billions.

- That pool buys businesses and assets. Not just any businesses — but ones that meet community needs and generate real profit.
- Profits are reinvested and distributed. Part goes back into the fund for growth. Part goes out to members as dividends.
- Everyone benefits. Owners, workers, families, children, the community at large.

This is the genius of the community mutual fund. It is not complex. It is not mystical. It is simple. And simplicity scales.

NLP Reframe — From Scarcity to Abundance

You may have been taught to believe, "I don't have enough." That is a scarcity mindset. But scarcity dissolves in the presence of strategy.

Close your eyes and repeat this with me:

"My small becomes significant. My little becomes large. My dollar becomes destiny."

As you breathe these words, notice how your body relaxes. Notice how hope stirs inside you. That is your subconscious letting go of the old lie — *"I don't have enough"* — and embracing the new truth: *"Together, we have more than enough."*

Historical Echoes

Black Wall Street in Tulsa, Oklahoma, once proved what collective economics could accomplish. Businesses, banks, theaters, and schools thrived — until violence and envy destroyed it. The lesson of Black Wall Street is not that it failed, but that it worked so well it was attacked.

WPBS is not a re-run of history; it is a resurrection of destiny. But this time, we will not be scattered. This time, we will not be unprotected. This time, we will be fortified by systems, by transparency, by scale.

The Guardrails of Trust

Trust is the currency that makes any mutual fund possible. Without trust, the system collapses. That is why WPBS will be built on transparency. Every dollar will be tracked. Every investment will be explained. Every dividend will be distributed fairly.

We will not be another scandal. We will not be another false promise. We will not be another pyramid scheme. WPBS is not built on hype. It is built on math, on systems, on ownership.

Biblical Blueprint

In Acts 2:44-45, the early church practiced a form of communal economics: "And all that believed were together, and had all things common; and sold their possessions and goods, and parted them to all men, as every man had need."

That was not poverty. That was power. That was unity. WPBS echoes that blueprint — not forced, not taxed, but voluntary, joyful, and visionary. We pool, we own, we share. And in doing so, we prove that unity is wealth.

From Wall Street to Our Street

For too long, Wall Street has prospered while our street has struggled. But Wall Street's principles are not magical — they are mathematical. They work because of scale, because of pooling, because of discipline.

And now it is our turn. We will not wait for permission. We will not wait for philanthropy. We will not wait for another politician's promise. We will create our own Wall Street — right here in West Philadelphia.

Subconscious Activation — See It Now

Imagine walking into a gas station, and the receipt prints at the bottom: Owned by WPBS. Owned by you. Imagine swiping your card at a supermarket, and knowing a portion of every dollar spent comes back to your community. Imagine paying rent in an apartment complex, and knowing you're not just a tenant — you're a shareholder.

See it. Feel it. Let it root in your subconscious. Because what you see internally, you will create externally.

Closing Declaration

Let us seal this chapter with a declaration:

- We are pooling our dollars.
- We are building our fortress.
- We are creating our own mutual fund.
- We are owners, not beggars.
- We are builders, not borrowers.
- We are part of a divine economy.

Say it until you believe it. Believe it until you act on it. Act on it until you see it. And see it until it becomes your children's inheritance.

This is our community mutual fund. This is WPBS. This is destiny at work.

Chapter 5
Businesses We Own Together

There is a sacred difference between a business that takes from you and a business that belongs to you. One drains you; the other sustains you. One steals your future; the other seeds your future. For too long, West Philadelphia has been filled with businesses that sit on our corners but not in our hearts. They profit from our presence but never invest in our prosperity.

But imagine with me: every store, every service, every building you see on your block could be ours. Owned by us. Staffed by us. Profiting us. Feeding our families. Funding our future. This is the vision of WPBS — businesses we own together.

The Cornerstore Problem

Walk down any street in West Philly and you'll find a corner store. Who owns it? Not us. Where do the profits go? Not here. Our children buy snacks, our elders buy groceries, our families spend their limited dollars — and at the end of the day, the cash drawer is emptied and carried away, gone from the neighborhood forever.

This is not accidental. It is economic colonization. When you do not own the store on your corner, you are paying rent to strangers with every dollar you spend. But WPBS says: No more. We will own the corner. We will own the commerce. We will own the cash flow.

Gas Stations — Fueling Our Own Future

Every car that drives needs fuel. But every gallon pumped today fills someone else's bank account. What if every gallon filled ours? WPBS gas stations will not just provide fuel for cars; they will fuel dreams. Each pump will be a fountain of community wealth.

When we own the gas station, we no longer watch millions of dollars leak out of our community. Instead, those millions circulate back — paying wages, funding dividends, building schools, healing hospitals.

Supermarkets & Mini-Marts — Feeding Ourselves

Food deserts kill communities. Too many of our neighborhoods are flooded with fast food and starved of fresh food. Owning supermarkets and mini-marts means we are no longer at the mercy of corporate chains that raise prices and lower standards.

Imagine walking into a community-owned supermarket where every purchase not only feeds your family but also grows your equity. Fresh produce, fair prices, owned by the very people who shop there. That's not just commerce — that's covenant.

Banks & Credit Unions — Financing Our Destiny

Money is power, but only if you control it. Right now, too many of our people are denied loans, trapped by predatory lenders, or forced into financial systems that strip wealth instead of building it.

WPBS will establish credit unions and community banks that see us not as risks, but as partners. Loans for businesses, mortgages for homes, credit for families — all funded by us, for us. No more begging for approval from institutions that never wanted us to succeed. Our dollars will finance our destiny.

Hospitals & Clinics — Healing Our Own

The healthcare crisis in our community is not just about sickness — it's about ownership. Hospitals charge us, but do not employ us. Clinics serve us, but do not belong to us.

Imagine a hospital where the board members are from the community, where the profits are reinvested into wellness programs, where the workers look like the patients, where every bill paid becomes part of a cycle of healing and empowerment. That's what happens when we own the institutions of healing.

Housing Developments — Building Roots, Not Just Roofs

Rent is another form of economic slavery when the landlords don't live in the neighborhood. Every rent check we write leaves our community like water leaking through a broken pipe.

But imagine WPBS-owned housing developments where tenants are also shareholders. Rent doesn't disappear — it circulates. Families aren't just renters — they are co-owners. Children aren't raised in someone else's investment — they are raised in their own inheritance.

Technology & Innovation — Owning the Future

If we don't own technology, we will forever rent the future. Apps, platforms, startups, green energy, artificial intelligence — these are not luxuries; they are the engines of tomorrow.

WPBS will invest in tech incubators, youth coding programs, renewable energy, and green jobs. Because the future will not wait for us — we must build it now. We will not be users only; we will be inventors, innovators, and investors.

Media Platforms — Controlling the Narrative

Every time you turn on the news, you see how stories about our communities are twisted, edited, sensationalized. Whoever controls the narrative controls the perception.

Owning media platforms means owning the microphone. We will broadcast our own news, publish our own stories, produce our own films, amplify our own voices. Our children will not grow up under the weight of stereotypes — they will grow up under the light of truth.

Entertainment & Culture — Profiting from Our Gift

From hip hop to fashion, from sports to art, the culture of our people is imitated worldwide. But how much of that money comes back to us? Very little.

WPBS will own recording studios, streaming platforms, sports facilities, and production companies. When our artists create, we will profit. When our athletes play, we will profit. When our culture shines, we will profit. Because our creativity is not free — it is priceless.

The Power of Togetherness

Now, you may be thinking, This is too big. Too much. Too far-fetched. But remember: no single one of us has to own it all. We own it together.

Alone, you might never buy a hospital. Together, we can. Alone, you might never open a bank. Together, we can. Alone, you might never build a supermarket. Together, we can.

This is the beauty of WPBS: you don't carry the mountain alone. We climb it shoulder to shoulder, step by step, dollar by dollar, business by business.

NLP Anchoring — See Yourself Inside

Take a moment right now and close your eyes. Picture yourself walking into a supermarket. The cashier smiles because she knows you're not just a customer — you're an owner. You swipe your card at the pump, and you know part of that transaction is coming back to you. You deposit money at the credit union, and you know you're not funding someone else's empire — you're funding your own.

See it. Feel it. Anchor it. Because what you vividly imagine, your subconscious will compel you to manifest.

Say it with me:

"We own the business. We own the block. We own the future."

Biblical Echo

Deuteronomy 28:12 says, "The Lord will open to you His good treasure… you shall lend to many nations, but you shall not borrow." Ownership is not optional; it is covenantal. To borrow forever is to live beneath the covenant. To own together is to rise into the covenant.

The children of Israel were told to inherit the land. Not lease it. Not rent it. Not beg for it. Inherit it. That is our call as well.

Closing Declaration

Let this chapter end not in theory but in declaration:

- We will own the gas stations.
- We will own the supermarkets.
- We will own the banks.
- We will own the hospitals.
- We will own the housing.
- We will own the technology.
- We will own the media.
- We will own the culture.

We will not just spend. We will not just consume. We will own.

Because ownership is not just about business — it is about dignity. And when we own together, we rise together.

Chapter 6
Dividends of Destiny

There is a powerful difference between being given something and being rewarded for what you own. A gift can bless you, but ownership transforms you. A handout can fill your stomach for a day, but a dividend fills your bank account, your confidence, your future.

A dividend is not charity. A dividend is proof. Proof that your investment worked. Proof that your ownership is real. Proof that your money, your voice, your faith, your dollar has a destiny.

And that, my friend, is what WPBS is designed to deliver: Dividends of Destiny.

What Is a Dividend?

In the language of Wall Street, a dividend is a distribution of profits to shareholders. It is the company's way of saying, "Thank you for owning with us. Here is your portion of the reward."

Now imagine that principle applied to our community. Every month, every quarter, every year — as WPBS businesses generate profit, those profits return to you, the shareholder. You are not just a customer, not just a worker, not just a resident. You are an owner. And owners get paid.

The Difference Between Charity and Ownership

For too long, we have been treated as objects of charity. Politicians toss crumbs and call it policy. Corporations donate pennies and call it partnership. Even our own hearts have been trained to look for handouts instead of ownership.

But hear me clearly: WPBS is not about charity. Charity is a bandage. Ownership is a cure. Charity gives you fish. Ownership teaches you how to run the pond. Charity may soothe your hunger, but ownership secures your harvest.

When you receive a WPBS dividend, it is not pity. It is power.

The Mathematics of Dividends

Let's break it down so the vision is undeniable.

- Imagine one WPBS-owned gas station earning $1 million in profit per year. After reinvestment, a portion of that profit is distributed to shareholders. That's money flowing back into the hands of the people who fueled the dream.

- Imagine ten supermarkets netting $50 million. A portion returns to the community shareholders as cash, while another portion is reinvested into new ventures.

- Imagine an entire hospital, owned by the people, generating sustainable income while also saving lives. Dividends flow not just in dollars, but in dignity — healthier bodies, longer lives, stronger families.

This is not fantasy. This is multiplication. This is destiny manifested in the form of checks and deposits.

NLP Anchoring — Feel It Now

Take a breath. Now imagine opening your bank app. You see a deposit notification. It reads: Dividend Payment — WPBS. Pause and feel that. Not a paycheck from an employer. Not a benefit from a government. But a dividend from your own community's collective wealth.

Say this with me:

"I am a shareholder. I receive dividends. My money multiplies. My future is secure."

Repeat it until you feel your posture shift, your spirit rise, your subconscious align. Because as you confess it, you begin to believe it. And what you believe, you pursue.

Beyond Dollars: The Dividend of Dignity

Yes, the checks matter. But the deeper dividend is what happens inside you. The dividend of dignity.

- When you hold that check, you feel pride.
- When you explain it to your children, you give them vision.
- When you spend it, you circulate prosperity, not pity.

The dividend of dignity tells you: You are not powerless. You are not forgotten. You are not waiting for rescue. You are building wealth with your own hands, your own faith, your own dollars.

A Story of Transformation

Imagine a single mother in West Philly — let's call her Keisha. She joins WPBS with her $1 a day. At first, it feels small. But months turn to years, and her investment grows. Then one day, she receives her first dividend payment. It's not millions, but it's enough to pay her light bill without stress. It's enough to cover groceries without sacrifice. It's enough to remind her that she is not alone, that she is part of something bigger.

That check is more than money — it is a lifeline. And as WPBS grows, so do the dividends. Keisha uses them to save, to invest, to send her daughter to college, to start a side business. All because she said yes to $1 a day.

Her dollar had a destiny. And that destiny paid her back.

Biblical Echo — Fruit That Remains

Jesus said, "I chose you and appointed you that you should go and bear fruit, and that your fruit should remain" (John 15:16). Dividends are the fruit of ownership. They remain long after the labor. They feed you long after the seed is planted.

Psalm 1 declares that the righteous man is like a tree planted by rivers of water, that brings forth fruit in season, whose leaf shall not wither — and whatever he does shall prosper.

Ownership is the planting. Dividends are the prospering.

Why Dividends Matter to the Subconscious

The subconscious mind craves evidence. It does not just want promises; it wants proof. Every time you receive a WPBS dividend, it is proof. Proof that collective economics works. Proof that your sacrifice produces fruit. Proof that you are not crazy to believe in a million-dollar dream.

This evidence rewires your subconscious. It shifts you from doubt to faith, from hesitation to confidence. With each dividend, you don't just grow richer — you grow bolder.

Reinvesting the Harvest

And here is the beauty: dividends don't just end with spending. They become seeds for reinvestment. As we receive, we give back. As we harvest, we sow again. As we profit, we expand.

This cycle of sowing and reaping is the divine rhythm of wealth. WPBS dividends ensure that rhythm never stops.

Subconscious Visualization — The Check in Your Hand

Pause. Picture this clearly. In your hand is a check. It has your name on it. It is signed by WPBS. The memo reads: Dividend Payment — Community Wealth. You feel its weight. You see its ink. You know its meaning.

Hold that image. Because what the mind rehearses, the body realizes.

Closing Declaration

Let us declare it boldly:

- We are shareholders.
- We receive dividends.
- Our money multiplies.
- Our dignity is restored.
- Our future is secure.

No longer will we settle for scraps. No longer will we live as renters in someone else's vision. We are owners. We are investors. We are receivers of dividends of destiny.

And those dividends will not just change our wallets. They will change our world.

Chapter 7
Generational Wealth Transfer

A tree does not eat its own fruit. A river does not drink its own water. And true wealth is never meant for one lifetime only. Wealth is not complete until it flows forward. Until it nourishes those who come after us. Until it plants seeds in fields we may never walk.

The greatest failure of our time has not been the lack of money in our hands, but the lack of inheritance in our children's hands. Too many of us live for survival instead of succession. Too many of us bury our potential with us when we die, leaving our children to start from zero, or worse, from debt.

But hear me clearly: WPBS is not about a quick fix. It is about a generational foundation. It is not about getting rich fast. It is about making our grandchildren rich in faith, in wisdom, in resources, in ownership. This is about generational wealth transfer.

The Biblical Mandate

The Word says: "A good man leaves an inheritance to his children's children" (Proverbs 13:22). Notice — not just to his children, but to his children's children. That means wealth must be planned three generations deep. If it dies with you, it was never wealth. It was wages. True wealth lives longer than your lifespan.

Psalm 112 declares: "His seed shall be mighty upon earth: the generation of the upright shall be blessed. Wealth and riches shall be in his house." That is not wishful thinking. That is covenant promise.

43

Arrows in the Hands of a Mighty Warrior

The Psalmist wrote: "Like arrows in the hands of a warrior are children born in one's youth. Blessed is the man whose quiver is full of them" (Psalm 127:4-5).

Think about that imagery. Arrows. An arrow is not meant to stay in the quiver. It is meant to fly further than the archer can reach. Our children are arrows. Wealth is the bow. Legacy is the aim. WPBS is the arm pulling back the string.

When we invest collectively, we are not just shooting for today. We are launching arrows into the future. Our children will go places we never walked. They will conquer territories we only dreamed of.

Breaking the Curse of "Starting Over"

How many times have we heard this story? A mother works two jobs, a father hustles to pay bills, and when they pass on, their children inherit nothing but debt. The cycle begins again: struggling, scraping, surviving. Every generation starting over at zero.

That cycle is a curse. And curses must be broken. WPBS exists to break it.

Imagine instead: parents invest $1 a day into WPBS. Over the years, it grows. Dividends flow. Assets are built. When they pass, their children inherit not debt but shares. Not bills but businesses. Not scarcity but stability. And those children don't start at zero — they start at ownership.

That is generational wealth transfer.

Education as Inheritance

Wealth is not just money. It is mindset. If you give your children money without wisdom, they will lose both. If you give them wisdom with money, they will multiply both.

WPBS will establish youth pipelines for financial literacy, entrepreneurship, coding, green energy, and business management. Our children must not only inherit wealth; they must inherit the skills to sustain and expand it.

This is why we must talk to our children now — around the dinner table, after church, in the car rides — about ownership, about investing, about discipline. Every conversation is a deposit. Every lesson is a dividend.

A Story of Legacy

Think of Jamal from Chapter 1. Imagine if, instead of his life ending, he had been raised in a system where his family owned assets, where he inherited not struggle but strategy. Imagine his children receiving not trauma but trust funds.

Now imagine multiplying that story by a million. That is the power of WPBS generational wealth transfer. Each life redeemed, each legacy restored, each arrow launched.

NLP Anchoring — See the Lineage

Close your eyes. Picture your grandchildren. Maybe you have them already, maybe you don't yet. See their faces — bright, strong, smiling. Now imagine handing them not just hugs and memories, but deeds, shares, dividends, and wisdom. Imagine saying: "This is yours. This is your inheritance. This is your legacy."

Say it now:

"I will not leave my children empty. I will not let my grandchildren start at zero. I am building wealth that will outlive me."

Let that affirmation sink into your subconscious. Every repetition is a brick in the wall of your family's future.

From Survival to Succession

Survival asks, "How will I make it today?" Succession asks, "What will I leave tomorrow?"

Survival eats the seed. Succession plants it. Survival consumes the harvest. Succession stores some for the next season. Survival is about me. Succession is about we.

WPBS shifts us from survival to succession. We are not just living; we are leaving. We are not just working; we are willing. We are not just consuming; we are constructing.

The Subconscious Power of Legacy

Do you know why generational wealth is so powerful? Because it changes not only your finances but your identity. A child raised in ownership walks differently. They sit in class differently. They negotiate differently. Their subconscious is trained to believe: "I am not broke. I am not begging. I am an owner."

And when the subconscious changes, the trajectory of life changes.

Biblical Echo — Abraham's Inheritance

God promised Abraham: "I will make you a great nation... and in you all the families of the earth shall be blessed" (Genesis 12:2-3). That promise was not just for Abraham; it was for Isaac, for Jacob, for Israel, for generations.

We are heirs of that promise. And through WPBS, we will make it visible again. Our inheritance will not be abstract. It will be tangible. It will be transferable. It will be undeniable.

Closing Declaration

Declare this with me, with conviction:

- I will not leave my children empty.
- I will not pass down debt, I will pass down dividends.
- I will not bury wealth, I will transfer it.
- My children are arrows.
- My grandchildren are heirs.
- My lineage will prosper.

This is not just about money. This is about destiny. And when destiny flows generationally, no curse, no system, no enemy can stop it.

This is generational wealth transfer. This is WPBS. This is legacy alive.

Chapter 8
From Streets to Systems

The streets have stories. They whisper at night, they scream in the daylight. They tell of hustlers chasing survival, of sirens echoing pain, of mothers praying their sons make it home alive. The streets of West Philadelphia have been both birthplace and burial ground. And for too long, we have let the streets dictate the system.

But I declare: no more.

We are not called to be captives of the streets. We are called to be architects of systems. Streets may raise us, but systems sustain us. Streets may wound us, but systems can heal us. The West Philadelphia Billionaires Society exists to move us from streets to systems.

The Trap of the Streets

Walk through any block and you'll see the trap: poverty, unemployment, drugs, despair. A young man stands on the corner not because he lacks ambition, but because he lacks access. A young woman hustles not because she lacks intelligence, but because she lacks opportunity.

The streets are a system of survival — but survival is not enough. Survival consumes; it does not create. Survival keeps us alive for today, but it kills tomorrow. And as long as we leave our children to be mentored by the streets, the cycle repeats.

The Cost of Crime

Let's face the numbers. Every shooting costs the city millions in emergency response, policing, courts, and incarceration. Every crime not only drains the victim but also the entire community. Violence lowers property values, chases away investment, increases insurance rates, and multiplies fear.

When Jamal was murdered in Chapter 1, we saw how one life lost multiplies into millions wasted. Multiply that by hundreds of homicides, thousands of assaults, tens of thousands of incarcerations — and you begin to see the streets as the most expensive system in America.

We are already paying the bill for broken systems. The question is: will we keep paying for death, or will we invest in life?

From Hustle to Enterprise

The truth is, many of our young people already have the skills of entrepreneurs. They know supply and demand. They understand marketing. They manage teams. They take risks. The problem is not their talent. The problem is their training.

The streets teach them how to build empires that collapse. WPBS will teach them how to build enterprises that last. Instead of hustling for pennies, they will build for profit. Instead of running from the law, they will write the law. Instead of fearing police, they will employ police in businesses they own.

We are not throwing our youth away. We are redirecting them from streets to systems.

Swords Into Plowshares

The prophet Isaiah declared: "They shall beat their swords into plowshares, and their spears into pruning hooks: nation shall not lift up sword against nation, neither shall they learn war any more" (Isaiah 2:4).

This is not just poetry. It is prophecy. Swords are weapons of destruction; plowshares are tools of production. The call is clear: turn your weapons into work. Turn your violence into value. Turn your pain into profit.

WPBS is the forge where swords become plowshares. Where the same hands that once gripped guns will grip contracts. Where the same minds that once plotted revenge will plot expansion. Where the same energy that once fueled crime will fuel creation.

The System of Opportunity

Imagine with me. A young man once arrested for hustling on the corner is now managing inventory at a WPBS supermarket. A young woman once trapped in cycles of poverty is now running her own salon funded by a WPBS microloan. A teenager once tempted by gangs is now coding apps in a WPBS technology lab.

This is what happens when systems replace streets. The cycle breaks. The curse lifts. The future shifts.

NLP Reframe — From Fear to Vision

Close your eyes. Picture your block at night. Instead of sirens, hear laughter. Instead of gunshots, hear music. Instead of corners filled with hustlers, see businesses filled with owners. Instead of fear, feel safety.

Now say this with me:

"My streets are changing. My system is rising. My future is secure."

Repeat it until your body believes it. Because your subconscious cannot tell the difference between vivid imagination and lived reality. And what you vividly imagine, you will subconsciously pursue.

Building Systems of Justice

But WPBS is not just about business. It is about justice. For too long, the justice system has been tilted against us — over-policing, mass incarceration, discriminatory sentencing. But when we own businesses, when we control capital, when we elect leaders, we begin to influence laws.

Justice is not only in the courtroom. Justice is in the paycheck. Justice is in the ownership papers. Justice is in the opportunities that keep a child in school instead of in jail.

From streets to systems means from injustice to equity.

A Story of Transformation

Meet Tyrone. At 16, he was arrested for dealing drugs. By 20, he had a record that made it nearly impossible to get a job. The streets claimed him as another statistic. But through WPBS, Tyrone receives training in logistics and supply chain management. He starts working at a community-owned warehouse. Within years, he's managing operations, earning dividends, mentoring youth.

Tyrone's story is not just his. It's a prophecy of what can happen when we invest in systems instead of punishing streets.

Biblical Echo — Joseph's System

Joseph was sold into slavery, betrayed by his brothers, locked in prison. But God gave him a vision — a system to store grain in times of plenty to survive times of famine (Genesis 41). That system not only saved Egypt; it saved nations.

We are Josephs in our time. Betrayed, enslaved, imprisoned, overlooked — but filled with God's wisdom to create systems that sustain. WPBS is our grain storehouse. WPBS is our survival strategy. WPBS is our salvation system.

Closing Declaration

Declare this with me:

- We are moving from streets to systems.
- We are turning swords into plowshares.
- We are shifting from fear to vision.
- We are building justice, not prisons.
- We are transforming hustlers into entrepreneurs.
- We are redeeming our streets through systems.

The streets have had their say. But now the systems will speak louder. And the systems we build will outlast bullets, outlive violence, and outshine despair.

This is the call of WPBS: from streets to systems, from pain to power, from survival to success.

Chapter 9
The Spiritual Blueprints

Before a builder lays the first brick, before a contractor pours the first foundation, before an architect draws the first line — there must be a blueprint. The blueprint is not the building, but without it, the building collapses. The blueprint is the invisible plan that makes the visible possible.

And so it is with the West Philadelphia Billionaires Society. WPBS is not merely an economic idea. It is not just social innovation. It is not simply community development. It is a spiritual blueprint. Heaven drew the design before we ever touched the pen.

Ownership Is Spiritual

The Bible begins with ownership. "The earth is the Lord's, and the fullness thereof" (Psalm 24:1). From the very first verse, we learn: everything belongs to God. And if we are His children, we are heirs — joint heirs with Christ (Romans 8:17).

Ownership is not greed; it is godly. Stewardship is not optional; it is obedience. To live without ownership is to live beneath a covenant. To claim ownership is to walk in alignment with heaven.

Multiplication Is Spiritual

The first command God gave humanity was this: "Be fruitful, and multiply, and replenish the earth, and subdue it" (Genesis 1:28). Fruitfulness is not a suggestion; it is a mandate. Multiplication is not an accident; it is a command.

When we multiply our dollars, our businesses, our influence, we are not doing something secular — we are obeying something sacred. WPBS is not just economics; it is obedience to the very first words God spoke to mankind.

The Parable of the Talents

Jesus told a story of three servants given talents (Matthew 25:14–30). One received five talents, one received two, and one received one. Two multiplied what they were given. One buried it in the ground.

The master returned and rewarded the multipliers, but called the one who buried his talent "wicked and lazy." Notice: the sin was not theft, not violence, not dishonesty — it was wasting potential.

Too many of us have buried our talents — our dollars, our skills, our ideas — in the ground of fear, the soil of scarcity, the grave of distraction. WPBS is the shovel that digs them back up. We will not bury another dollar. We will multiply. We will invest. We will increase. Because heaven rewards multiplication.

The Acts Blueprint

The early church in Acts 2:44–45 provides a model: "And all that believed were together, and had all things common; and sold their possessions and goods, and parted them to all men, as every man had need."

This was not socialism. This was not communism. This was kingdom. A divine economy where believers pooled resources, met needs, and advanced the gospel.

WPBS echoes that same principle — voluntary, joyful, intentional pooling of resources for collective prosperity. This is not theory. This is Scripture reborn in strategy.

The Storehouse Principle

Malachi 3:10 commands: "Bring all the tithes into the storehouse, that there may be food in My house, and try Me now in this, says the Lord of hosts, if I will not open for you the windows of heaven and pour out for you such blessing that there will not be room enough to receive it."

The storehouse was God's system of collective provision. Everyone brought in, so that no one went without. WPBS is a modern-day storehouse. Each dollar is seed in the storehouse. Each dividend is proof of the blessing. Each business we own is heaven's storehouse open on earth.

NLP Reframe — Wealth as Worship

You've been taught money is worldly. You've been told ownership is selfish. You've been conditioned to believe that holiness equals poverty. But that is a lie of the enemy.

Say this with me:

"My wealth is worship. My stewardship is sacred. My ownership is obedience."

Feel how different that sounds in your spirit. Wealth is not sin. Wealth without purpose is sin. But wealth aligned with God's will is worship.

The Battle in the Spirit

Make no mistake: poverty is not just economic. It is spiritual warfare. The enemy uses debt to shackle, lack to discourage, crime to destroy, scarcity to divide.

But the weapons of our warfare are not carnal; they are mighty through God. WPBS is not only about fighting poverty in the bank

— it is about breaking strongholds in the spirit. Every business we build, every dividend we pay, every family we lift is a blow against the enemy's kingdom.

This is why WPBS will be fought. Systems of oppression will resist it. Spirits of greed will attack it. But the gates of hell shall not prevail against a people who know they are building on a spiritual blueprint.

A Kingdom Economy

The kingdom of God has always had its own economy. In the wilderness, God sent manna daily. In the promised land, He gave them vineyards they didn't plant and houses they didn't build (Deuteronomy 6:11). In the New Testament, Jesus fed multitudes with five loaves and two fish.

The kingdom economy multiplies little into much. It turns scarcity into surplus. It turns slaves into stewards. And WPBS is a reflection of that kingdom economy on earth.

Subconscious Visualization — Heaven's Drafting Table

Close your eyes for a moment. Picture heaven as an architect's studio. See God unrolling a great blueprint on the table. On that blueprint are drawn businesses, schools, hospitals, banks, media platforms. And written at the top in bold letters: West Philadelphia Billionaires Society.

Now imagine the Lord placing the pen in your hand and saying: "Build what I have already designed."

Say it now:

"I am building God's blueprint. I am fulfilling heaven's plan. I am aligned with divine design."

When your subconscious embraces this truth, your doubt dissolves. You no longer ask "Can we?" You declare "We must."

The Prophetic Picture

Imagine a Sunday morning in West Philadelphia, twenty years from now. Churches are full, hospitals are owned by us, children walk into schools we fund, families shop in supermarkets we own. During service, the pastor announces: "This month's WPBS dividends have been distributed." People shout not because they got a handout, but because they got a harvest.

That is not fantasy. That is the prophetic picture of the spiritual blueprint manifest in reality.

Closing Declaration

Let us declare it together:
- We are builders on heaven's blueprint.
- Ownership is obedience.
- Multiplication is mandate.
- Wealth is worship.
- Stewardship is sacred.
- WPBS is a kingdom strategy.

This is bigger than economics. This is spiritual. And because it is spiritual, it is unstoppable.

Chapter 10
Governance Without Corruption

Power without accountability is poison. Wealth without integrity is a curse. History shows us: empires have fallen, movements have crumbled, and revolutions have betrayed their people not because of lack of vision, but because of lack of governance.

The West Philadelphia Billionaires Society is too holy, too precious, too generational to be corrupted by greed, hijacked by egos, or destroyed by secrecy. If WPBS is to succeed, it must be governed with the same power it preaches: transparency, accountability, and righteousness.

Why Governance Matters

The Bible says: "Where no counsel is, the people fall: but in the multitude of counsellors there is safety" (Proverbs 11:14). Governance is not about control — it is about counsel. It is not about domination — it is about direction. Without governance, money is mismanaged, opportunities are wasted, trust is betrayed.

But with righteous governance, money multiplies, opportunities expand, trust deepens, and legacy endures.

Guardrails Against Greed

Every great movement has faced the temptation of greed. Leaders who begin with vision sometimes fall into corruption. Systems that begin with transparency often drift into secrecy.

WPBS must be different. We will establish guardrails that ensure every dollar is tracked, every investment is explained, every dividend is distributed fairly. No hidden ledgers. No secret deals. No shadow hands.

When the people invest, the people deserve to see.

Transparency as Currency

Trust is the most valuable currency in any movement. If people do not trust, they will not invest. If people do not trust, they will not stay. If people do not trust, they will not pass it to the next generation.

That is why WPBS will operate with radical transparency. Quarterly reports will not be hidden in boardrooms; they will be shared with members. Every shareholder will know where their dollar went, what it produced, and how it multiplied.

Transparency will be our shield. Integrity will be our insurance.

Biblical Echo — Moses and Jethro's Counsel

Even Moses, the great leader of Israel, faced the weight of governance. Jethro, his father-in-law, told him: "The thing that you do is not good. You will surely wear away... Provide out of all the people able men, such as fear God, men of truth, hating covetousness; and place such over them" (Exodus 18:17–21).

Notice the qualities: fear God, men of truth, hating covetousness. WPBS governance will not be for the greedy. It will be for the godly. Not for the power-hungry, but for the servant-hearted.

Community Boards, Not Dictators

This is not one man's empire. This is one million people's inheritance. WPBS governance will be structured with community boards, elected representatives, financial experts, and spiritual advisors. Decisions will not be made behind closed doors, but in the open.

Leadership will rotate. Accountability will be constant. Authority will be shared. Because ownership without accountability is dictatorship. And we are building destiny, not dynasties.

NLP Reframe — From Suspicion to Trust

Our people have been burned before. We have seen scams, schemes, and lies dressed up as salvation. The subconscious remembers betrayal, and it whispers: "Don't trust them. Don't believe them. They'll steal it too."

But repeat this with me:

"This time is different. This vision is righteous. This system is transparent. This destiny is ours."

Say it until the suspicion loosens its grip. Because the mind needs new anchors. And WPBS will provide not just words, but evidence to anchor trust.

Guarded by Systems

Governance without systems is chaos. WPBS will employ the best of technology: blockchain transparency, digital ledgers, open-source reporting. The same tools used to protect billions on Wall Street will protect billions on our street.

This is not just about faith; it is about systems. Faith without works is dead. Vision without systems is doomed.

Accountability in Action

Imagine this: every quarter, members receive a digital report showing profits, losses, reinvestments, and dividends. Charts. Graphs. Clarity. No smoke. No mirrors.

Imagine open forums where members can question leaders. Imagine whistleblower protections to prevent corruption. Imagine financial audits conducted not once a decade, but constantly.

This is governance without corruption. And it will be the backbone of WPBS.

A Story of Contrast

Think of the movements that collapsed under the weight of greed. Leaders who lived lavishly while their people stayed poor. Organizations that promised change but delivered chains.

Now imagine WPBS as the opposite. Leaders who live simply. Systems that function transparently. Communities that actually prosper. This contrast will be our testimony. When skeptics ask, "How do you know it's real?" we will show them the proof.

Biblical Echo — The Watchmen

Ezekiel 33 describes the watchman: "Son of man, I have made you a watchman… if the watchman sees the sword coming and does not blow the trumpet, the blood will I require at the watchman's hand."

Our governance will have watchmen — financial watchmen, spiritual watchmen, community watchmen. Their job is not to dominate, but to protect. Not to exploit, but to warn. Not to profit alone, but to preserve the whole.

Subconscious Visualization — The Lighthouse

Close your eyes. Picture WPBS as a lighthouse. The storm is raging, the seas are rough, but the light cuts through the dark. Ships that once would have crashed on the rocks now find safe harbor. That lighthouse is governance. That light is transparency. That harbor is trust.

Say this with me:

"Our governance is our guard. Our systems are our shield. Our integrity is our inheritance."

Let your subconscious hold onto that image. Because when storms come — and they will — our lighthouse will stand.

Closing Declaration

Declare it boldly:

- We will govern with righteousness.
- We will lead with transparency.
- We will build systems that protect.
- We will not be corrupted.
- We will not be hijacked.
- We will not be destroyed by greed.

WPBS will not collapse like other movements. It will endure because it is governed. It will last because it is transparent. It will prosper because it is righteous.

This is governance without corruption. This is how we build not just for today, but for generations.

Chapter 11
Scaling Beyond Philadelphia

Every great fire begins with a spark. Every mighty river begins with a stream. Every global movement begins with a single city bold enough to believe. West Philadelphia is our spark. But the flame must not stay here. It must spread until it lights up every community hungry for freedom, equity, and ownership.

WPBS is not just for one neighborhood, not just for one zip code, not just for one city. It is a model, a prototype, a divine pattern that can be replicated. What we build here will be a blueprint for the world.

The Pattern Principle

The Lord told Moses: "See that you make everything according to the pattern shown you on the mountain" (Exodus 25:40). Moses' tabernacle was not meant to stay in the wilderness; it was a portable pattern, a moving system.

In the same way, WPBS is a pattern. It is a system of pooling, owning, governing, and prospering. Once established in West Philadelphia, it can be lifted, replicated, and planted in other cities, other nations, other continents.

This is not just a local movement. It is a global strategy.

From Philadelphia to Detroit

Detroit knows the story of economic collapse. Once the beating heart of America's auto industry, it became a cautionary tale of

67

disinvestment and decline. But Detroit also knows resilience. Imagine WPBS Detroit: community-owned auto repair shops, green energy firms, housing co-ops breathing new life into abandoned neighborhoods.

From West Philly's spark to Detroit's rebuild, the flame grows.

From Philadelphia to Baltimore

Baltimore carries scars much like ours — poverty, violence, disinvestment. But it also carries the spirit of resistance, creativity, and grit. WPBS Baltimore could transform vacant rowhouses into community-owned housing, turn boarded-up stores into thriving co-ops, channel billions into schools instead of prisons.

Philadelphia and Baltimore — sister cities, sister stories, sister solutions.

From Philadelphia to Chicago

Chicago's South and West Sides have been demonized for crime, but beneath the headlines are families, churches, and young people desperate for opportunity. WPBS Chicago could channel collective dollars into tech hubs, credit unions, and healthcare centers — turning the "windy city" into a wealth-building city.

Imagine a million-dollar-a-day movement not just healing, but transforming Chicago block by block.

From Philadelphia to Kingston, Accra, and Beyond

And then, beyond America's borders. Kingston, Jamaica — where reggae was born and resilience thrives. Accra, Ghana — a city of history, hustle, and hope. Lagos, Nigeria — a megacity bursting with youthful energy. Port-au-Prince, Haiti — battered yet unbroken.

What if WPBS became not just a local fund, but a diaspora fund? Imagine African Americans, Caribbeans, and Africans uniting across oceans — pooling dollars, pounds, cedis, naira — building hospitals in Ghana, schools in Jamaica, housing in Haiti, tech hubs in Nigeria.

A million voices in Philadelphia joined by a million in Kingston, a million in Lagos, a million in Accra. This is not just economics. This is a pan-African resurrection.

The Diaspora Dividend

When the children of Africa unite financially, nothing can stop us. For too long, the diaspora has been divided — separated by language, borders, and colonizers' lines. But money speaks one language. Ownership speaks one language. Prosperity speaks one language.

WPBS can be the bridge. From Philadelphia to the world, we will prove: Black wealth is not only possible — it is unstoppable.

NLP Reframe — See the Expansion

Take a deep breath. Now imagine pulling up a map. Place your finger on West Philadelphia. See the spark glow bright. Now watch as lines of fire stretch from Philly to Detroit, Baltimore, Chicago, Kingston, Accra, Lagos. Each city lights up like stars on a dark canvas. One by one, the constellation forms.

Say this with me:

"From one spark to many flames. From one city to many nations. From one people to a global family."

Your subconscious just rehearsed the expansion. What it rehearses, it will pursue.

The Global Echo

Jesus said: "You shall be witnesses unto Me in Jerusalem, and in all Judea and Samaria, and to the uttermost parts of the earth" (Acts 1:8). Notice the pattern: local, regional, global. Start where you are. Then expand. Then multiply until the world hears the witness.

West Philadelphia is our Jerusalem. Detroit, Baltimore, Chicago are our Judea and Samaria. Kingston, Accra, Lagos are our uttermost parts of the earth. The WPBS witness will not stay small. It will echo across oceans.

Systems That Scale

Scaling is not just about vision; it is about systems. The WPBS model will be packaged — the governance structures, the pooling mechanisms, the dividend distributions, the business ownership models — so any city can adopt the blueprint.

This is how franchises work. This is how corporations expand. And if McDonald's can sell burgers worldwide, WPBS can build wealth worldwide.

A Story of Multiplication

Picture this: ten years from now, a young woman in Accra attends a WPBS Ghana meeting. She invests her one cedi a day. At the same time, a young man in Detroit invests his dollar. A grandmother in Kingston invests her hundred Jamaican dollars. A father in Philadelphia invests his dollar.

Though thousands of miles apart, they are connected in one system, one vision, one dividend. When profits return, they do not just receive money — they receive proof that they are part of something global.

Closing Declaration

Declare it with me:

• WPBS is a pattern.
• WPBS is a blueprint.
• What begins in Philadelphia will not end in Philadelphia.
• From Philly to Detroit, from Baltimore to Chicago, from Kingston to Accra to Lagos — we are uniting.
• We are one people.
• We are one movement.
• We are one destiny.

This is bigger than a city. This is bigger than a country. This is bigger than us. This is the sound of a global awakening.

WPBS is not just a local revolution. It is a worldwide resurrection.

Chapter 12
The Call of A Million Voices

Close your eyes for a moment and listen. Can you hear it? It starts faint, like a whisper carried on the wind. One voice, then another. A mother praying. A father declaring. A child dreaming. A student studying. A worker hustling.

Now the sound grows. From porches to pulpits, from classrooms to corner stores, from prisons to pews. The whisper becomes a chorus. The chorus becomes a roar. And soon, it is unmistakable: the sound of a million voices rising as one.

This is not noise. This is not chaos. This is the call of a million voices.

The Power of Unity

One voice can inspire. Ten voices can motivate. A thousand voices can shake a city. But a million voices? A million voices can shift the earth.

Ecclesiastes 4:12 says: "Though one may be overpowered, two can defend themselves. A cord of three strands is not quickly broken." If two are powerful, and three are stronger, then what about one million bound together in covenant? That is unbreakable. That is unstoppable. That is unshakable.

The call of a million voices is not just noise; it is power in harmony.

Why a Million?

You may ask: why one million? Why not a thousand? Why not ten thousand? Because numbers are not just math; they are movement.

One million voices means one million testimonies. One million streams flowing into one river. One million investors, one million prayer warriors, one million activists, one million builders.

And let us be clear: this is not just about raising dollars. It is about raising destiny. The million is symbolic of fullness, of completion, of strength that cannot be silenced.

The Subconscious Echo

As you read these words, I want you to feel something stir in your chest. That is not coincidence. That is your spirit resonating with destiny. The subconscious loves repetition, so let me anchor this in you now:

Say it with me three times:

"I am one of the million.

I am one of the million.

I am one of the million."

Each time you say it, your mind believes it more. Each time you declare it, your subconscious aligns deeper. You are not watching history. You are writing it.

The Mobilization of the Masses

Imagine a rally in West Philadelphia. Thousands gathered in a stadium, lifting their voices. Cameras rolling. Media covering. And across the screen, the message flashes: One million strong. One dollar a day. One destiny together.

From that rally, people go home and sign up. Churches announce it from pulpits. Schools teach it in classrooms. Barbershops talk about it in chairs. Grandmothers tell grandchildren about it at the kitchen table. The mobilization spreads like fire.

This is how movements are born. Not in secret meetings, but in the open roar of the people.

A Call to Every Sector

The call of a million voices is not limited. It summons:

- The Church: Preach ownership as obedience, stewardship as worship, prosperity as promise.
- The Schools: Teach financial literacy, entrepreneurship, coding, wealth creation.
- The Families: Talk around the table about inheritance, about ownership, about destiny.
- The Streets: Transform hustlers into entrepreneurs, survivors into builders.
- The Elders: Share wisdom, history, and guidance to steer the movement right.
- The Youth: Bring energy, creativity, innovation, and boldness.

Every voice matters. Every role counts. Every sector must rise.

The Sound of Agreement

Amos 3:3 asks: "Can two walk together, except they be agreed?" The power is not just in speaking, but in agreeing.

The call of a million voices is not a million scattered cries. It is one cry, in agreement: Enough is enough. No more poverty. No more powerlessness. No more wasted generations. We will own. We will build. We will prosper.

Agreement is the amplifier. Agreement is the miracle. Agreement is the movement.

NLP Visualization — The Roar of the Million

Close your eyes again. Imagine standing in a stadium with one million people. Feel the vibration of their voices shaking the ground beneath your feet. Hear the roar echoing off the sky. Smell the sweat, the fire, the energy of the crowd. Now imagine your own voice joining theirs. You shout until your throat burns, but you know it's worth it, because you are part of something eternal.

Say it now:

"My voice matters. My voice is one of a million. My voice will not be silent."

Anchor that image in your subconscious. Because the more vividly you feel it, the more urgently you will live it.

A Story of the Million

Picture this: Keisha from Chapter 6, Tyrone from Chapter 8, Jamal's sister from Chapter 1 — all standing in that stadium. Around them are elders and youth, pastors and teachers, workers and entrepreneurs. Each one carries a different story, a different scar, a different strength. But together, they lift one sound.

This is not fiction. This is prophecy. And prophecy must be fulfilled.

The Global Chorus

And here's the wonder: it will not stop at Philadelphia. As we saw in Chapter 11, the million voices will be joined by millions more — in Detroit, in Baltimore, in Chicago, in Kingston, in Accra, in Lagos. Soon, the sound will not be a city's roar. It will be a global chorus.

And nations will take notice. Governments will ask questions. Corporations will tremble. Because the people, united in ownership, are louder than any system built to silence them.

Closing Declaration

Lift your voice now, wherever you are, and declare it with me:

- I am one of the million.
- My dollar has a destiny.
- My voice has power.
- My agreement has weight.
- I will not be silent.
- I will not be passive.
- I am part of the movement.
- I am part of the miracle.

This is the call of a million voices. And together, our sound will shake the heavens, shift the earth, and secure our destiny.

The Dream Realized

Close your eyes and let me take you forward. Twenty years from now. It's a bright morning in West Philadelphia. The sun is shining down on clean streets, bustling shops, laughter echoing from children on their way to schools that we built. The smell of fresh bread drifts from a community-owned bakery. The hum of electric buses, owned by our cooperative, glides past.

A grandmother sits on her porch, watching her grandchildren run freely, safely, joyfully. She remembers the days when gunshots interrupted sleep, when funerals outnumbered graduations, when poverty was the expectation. She smiles because those days are gone.

She knows why.

The Streets Have Changed

The corners that once sold death now sell opportunity. The abandoned lots are now gardens and playgrounds. The corner stores are WPBS-owned mini-marts. The gas stations fuel not just cars, but futures. The hospitals heal without draining pockets. The banks loan with dignity. The schools teach not just history, but ownership.

The streets have been redeemed. And it all began with a dollar a day.

Families Have Changed

Inside homes, children grow up hearing words like "dividend," "equity," and "ownership." Fathers are present, mothers are thriving, grandparents are smiling. Instead of handing down debt, families hand down deeds. Instead of telling stories of struggle, they tell stories of legacy.

Generational curses have been broken. Generational blessings are flowing. Families walk taller, think broader, dream bigger.

Systems Have Changed

The justice system no longer hunts our children. The healthcare system no longer ignores our pain. The economic system no longer bleeds our pockets dry. Because we built our own systems — systems that serve, systems that protect, systems that prosper.

Where once the system worked against us, now the system works for us.

The Global Connection

And it didn't stop in Philadelphia. Detroit rose. Baltimore thrived. Chicago transformed. Kingston rebuilt. Accra flourished. Lagos exploded with innovation. A global network of community-owned mutual funds now stretches across continents, uniting the African diaspora in unprecedented wealth and unity.

Our voices became one global chorus. Our dollars became one global river. Our destiny became one global reality.

The Prophetic Fulfillment

Remember Jamal from Chapter 1? In this future, there are no more Jamals lost to the streets. His name has become a memorial, not of tragedy, but of transformation. His story became the fuel that birthed the movement. And his sister, once broken by grief, now stands as a board member of WPBS, overseeing youth mentorship programs that have saved thousands of lives.

What was once pain has become prophecy fulfilled.

NLP Anchoring — See Yourself There

Now pause. Imagine yourself in this future. See yourself walking into a WPBS supermarket, paying with your debit card, knowing the profits return to you. See yourself attending a shareholder's meeting, voting on where to invest next. See yourself explaining to your grandchildren how you were one of the first to believe, one of the first to invest, one of the first to join the million.

Say it now:

"I am part of the dream. I am part of the legacy. I am part of the miracle."

Repeat it. Let it sink. Let it root in your subconscious. Because the more vividly you see it, the more urgently you will build it.

The Dream Realized

The West Philadelphia Billionaires Society is not just an idea. It is not just a book. It is a blueprint for destiny.

And the dream is not waiting for tomorrow. The dream begins now. With you. With me. With us. With one dollar a day. With one million voices. With one unstoppable vision.

West Philadelphia will no longer be known only for its struggles. It will be known as the birthplace of a movement that transformed a people, a nation, and a world.

The dream is real. The dream is realized. The dream is waiting for you to take your place.

Final Declaration

Stand wherever you are. Lift your voice and declare it:

- I am one of the million.
- I am an owner, not a beggar.
- I am a builder, not a borrower.
- I am a steward, not a slave.
- My dollar has a destiny.
- My voice has a sound.
- My future has a promise.
- My children will inherit wealth, not debt.
- My community will prosper, not perish.

This is the West Philadelphia Billionaires Society.

This is the dream realized.

This is your invitation.

Aaron Maxwell Montague

Aaron M. Montague, MBA, MDiv, PNLP, PTT, CCHt, CSC

Aaron M. Montague is a preacher, strategist, and builder of people who believes that ordinary folks—when united by vision, discipline, and love—can create extraordinary change. As the visionary mind behind the West Philadelphia Billionaires Society (WPBS), he champions a bold, simple idea: one million people, one dollar a day, building community-owned wealth that cannot be outsourced, gentrified away, or stolen by neglect.

A retired U.S. Armed Forces veteran with over twenty-one years of combined service in the Army and Navy, Aaron learned leadership, discipline, and sacrifice the hard way—under pressure, under orders, and often under commitment. After military retirement, he continued serving others as a certified Veterans Appeals advocate with a nationally recognized Veterans Service Organization, fighting to ensure that those who bore the battle receive the care and benefits they earned. That same warrior spirit now fuels his fight for economic justice, neighborhood ownership, and generational prosperity.

Aaron is the founder of Montague Motivational Ministries (MX3), where he blends his training in business (MBA), theology (MDiv), and transformational change (PNLP, PTT, CCHt, CSC) to empower believers, leaders, and everyday people to renew their minds, heal their stories, and rebuild their financial foundations. As a life coach, Bible teacher, and trance therapist, he speaks to both the conscious and subconscious mind—challenging limiting beliefs while igniting faith, vision, and action.

At the heart of Aaron's work is a simple conviction: we are not powerless, and we are not for sale. Through WPBS, he casts a prophetic, practical blueprint for turning scattered dollars into concentrated power—investing in gas stations, mini-marts, housing, healthcare, education, and more, all under community ownership. His writing weaves Scripture, street-level wisdom, financial literacy, and a fierce love for Black and Brown communities into a call-to-action that is as spiritual as it is strategic.

Aaron is a husband, father, grandfather, mentor, and spiritual coach to many. Whether he is preaching in a pulpit, coaching leaders in a boardroom, or sketching out community investment models on a napkin, his message remains the same: You were not born just to survive in someone else's system. You were created to build, own, and steward the Kingdom impact God has placed in your hands.

The West Philadelphia Billionaires Society is more than a book to him—it is a blueprint, a battle plan, and a love letter to communities that have been overlooked, underestimated, and under-capitalized for far too long.